HARLEY-DAVIDSON ELECTRA GLIDE

Malcolm Birkitt

First published in Great Britain in 1994
by Osprey, an imprint of Reed Consumer
Books Limited, Michelin House,
81 Fulham Road, London SW3 6RB and
Auckland, Melbourne, Singapore and Toronto.

ISBN 1 85532 402 4

Editor Shaun Barrington
Page design Paul Kime/Ward Peacock
Partnership

Printed and bound in Hong Kong
Produced by Mandarin Offset

Half title page
*Just the tool for long, straight roads
that stretch off to the horizon. It'll
probably climb the side of the mountain
too if you ask it*

Title page
*With unerring straight-line stability
and protected by that stylish handlebar
fairing, an Electra Glide rider can
climb aboard in the morning, head for
the horizon and still feel fresh come
dusk several hundred miles later*

Right
*Riding through monumental landscapes
– that's what's on this Electra Glide
owner's mind. Because there's lots of
fibreglass on the bike, there's plenty of
space to add a little custom paint*

For a catalogue of all books published by Osprey Automotive
please write to:

**The Marketing Department, Reed Consumer Books,
1st Floor, Michelin House, 81 Fulham Road, London SW3 6RB**

HARLEY-DAVIDSON
ELECTRA GLIDE

Contents

An impression of the dazzle on Main Street, Daytona Beach

Introduction

Back in 1965, the sole remaining USA motorcycle manufacturer wheeled out the first version of what has since become a touring legend. They called it the Electra Glide — two words and four syllables which even three decades on still sends a shiver down the spine.

We're talking, of course, about a large, American-sized motorcycle with big fat tyres at each end of its long 61 inch wheelbase, a mighty, elemental V-twin engine of enormous torque, and all the comforts and necessities for two-up travelling built in. That massively strong, slow revving motor with its tractor-like torque was just the thing for rolling

Above
A couple on an FLHS enjoy a quieter moment by a lake in the Black Hills, away from the hubbub of Main Street, Sturgis

Left
In the quest for better breathing, many owners bolt a different carb or air cleaner onto the V-twin

across as many state borders as you wished, without a dip in performance no matter how much gear was carried.

The machine in question was then, and still is now, more than just a mere motorcycle – it's a genuine icon of American values and sensibilities. The British designer Richard Seymour admirably summed up Harley's finest during a TV programme shown in Britain recently. Standing alongside an Electra Glide and holding his hand at a horizontal plane just below seat level, he said the machine's design seemed to be 'Roy Rogers from here up, and Union Pacific from here down.' Those emotive images of riding across sun-baked plains on a clanking, throbbing iron horse were conjured up for all who watched.

In my dog-eared copy of *Zen and the Art of Motorcycle Maintenance*, written in 1974, Robert M Pirsig also went straight to the heart of what riding a motorcycle, as opposed to riding in a car, is all about. 'On a cycle the frame is gone. You're completely in contact with it. You're in the scene, not just watching it anymore, and the sense of presence is overwhelming. That concrete whizzing by five inches below your foot is

Above
If you can't afford the bike, the least you can do is buy the T-shirt!

Right
The Black Hills' canyons echo to the sound of Harleys as this Electra Glide leads a small posse back towards Sturgis

the real thing, the same stuff you walk on, it's right there, so blurred you can't focus on it'

For many, then, the Electra Glide represents the quintessential Harley-Davidson, and its gleaming chrome and paint scheme somehow symbolising the 'American Dream'; others have utilised the practicalities of its fully dressed packaging to build a way of life out on the open road; yet more have been swayed by the V-twin's unique rumble, fired up by a fancy electric starter, of course. You too can own a H-D tourer and be a bandana'd rebel, even if it's only at weekends.

Harley-Davidson's 'King of the Road' has been elevated to an emblem of freedom, and an icon of American mythology to rank up alongside the Statue of Liberty, the Empire State, the Stars and Stripes and good old Mom's apple pie. The Harley cult really exploded in the 1980s and continues unabated as we rush towards the millennium. Right now a Harley-Davidson Electra Glide is like an icon of America, which says a lot about the way people can deify artefacts.

Above
Even in silhouette, there's no mistaking the Electra Glide's curvaceous fairing

Right
Some people will do anything for attention. Flames are often painted on petrol tanks but this guy's fanned them across the whole bike

It also makes you wonder about the wondrous abilities of the human imagination – after all, those early 'Glides were far from perfect. That much vaunted 'electric leg' tended not to want to crank the massive pistons into life if there was a hint of moisture in the air. The venerable Panhead mill itself had been rolling down American highways since 1948, and even then it was a descendant of the Knucklehead of 1936. And far from being an ideal touring machine, the Electra Glide had limited toting capacity, was ponderous around corners and had seriously modest braking.

Despite these dynamic and mechanical shortcomings, Harley's tourer immediately burrowed its way into our affections, and we've been hooked on the darn things ever since. This book looks at the way the Electra Glide came to be, the ups and downs of its thirty year life and its slow, sometimes painful evolution into a machine of the modern era, albeit an anachronistic one.

Above
Sidecar Electra Glides are a rarity, but have featured on and off in the range through the years, including a police spec model. This is a CLE from 1979 with three 16 inch cast alloy wheels and a low-geared 1340cc Shovelhead

Right
According to Harley-Davidson's research released in 1991, under 2% of FL owners are female

In 1965 the addition of an electric starter to the big twin motor gave rise to the Electra Glide moniker and thirty years later, the latest versions differ little from that original concept. Over the years Harley's engineers have only brought new technologies to bear where and when they felt there was a significant advantage to be gained.

The Electra Glide reminds us of what the motorcycle touring scene was like before the Honda Gold Wing came along and completely changed the rules. The Harley sets greater store by a set of traditional criteria that deal with the more human elements of touring – with sensations and emotions rather than pure efficiency and outright performance.

Flawed the bike may be, but there's no doubting its character. That sit-up-and-beg riding position is what they call an acquired taste, seemingly designed for someone about 6 inches below average height and with an unnaturally broad pelvis to span that wide motor and protruding air cleaner. The plush seat isn't that high but the width of the machine means even six-footers have to stretch a bit to balance the bike at rest.

Above
The owners of this 1979 CLE have added some neat custom paint to the original tan and creme

Left
Cowpokes used to tie their steeds up outside their favourite watering holes, and now the city slickers do the same with their iron horses

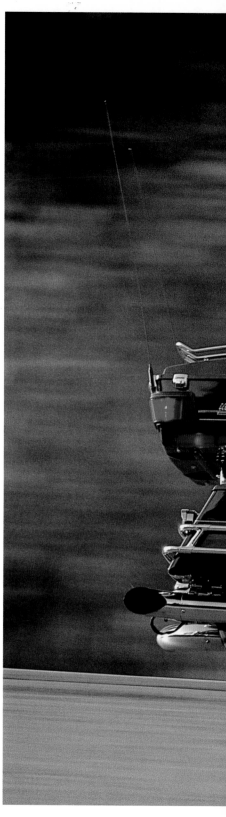

These aren't gripes – just observations, because that's the way big Harleys have always been.

The current H-D air-cooled 1340cc V-Twin redlines at a mere 5100rpm. Its design can be traced back for decades, and, while for the last fifteen years it's been held in place by a system of rubber mounts that isolate most of the engine's vibration from the rest of the bike, you can still sense that unique bump and thump going on below. There's no doubting the fact that you're sitting astride a real motorcycle, with a real engine and real character.

The venerable V-twins that have powered Harleys for almost 90 years, and the Electra Glide across four decades, may have become more sophisticated with time, but hardly more complicated. Compare that with the intricacy of any modern Japanese large capacity, multi-cylinder engine! For many the Harley's principal rival – the Gold Wing – is so refined as to be virtually car-like, and this reduces the pleasures of riding.

Harley riders prefer their motorcycles to be exactly that – not some two-wheeled development of a car. So the Electra Glide sports a quirky little

Above
Sturgis is a place where cool dudes with cool boxes congregate

Right
The 1993 Ultra Classic Electra Glide is big and beefy enough to accommodate any size or shape of pilot

fairing which gives moderate protection, ineffective leg shields on the luxury models, confusing handlebar controls, compromised luggage capacity and performance which remains stuck in the slow lane. In other words, it isn't nearly as sophisticated or integrated a piece, but it always manages to make an owner grin. It's an elemental motorcycle, or an earthy one depending on your opinion. Bikes are supposed to be fun to ride and the Electra Glide clearly is.

You could say that Harley chose to compete with the Japanese in a canny way – by not competing! The Electra Glide remains a motorcycle steeped in tradition and one that stirs the emotions – you either love it for what it is, or hate it for exactly the same reasons. There's no middle ground with the 'King of the Road' and long may it be that way.

The story told here – how Harley made significant functional changes to the Electra Glide without straying too far from its traditions – has one

Above
On his days off, this Houston Patrolman likes to get away from his weekday FLHTP mount, so he rides an FLHS instead. Here he leads an outing of the Hou-Tex chapter of the Harley Owners Group

Right
Main Street, Sturgis is where two-wheelers rule the roost each August. All that gleaming chrome and the kaleidoscope of colour hurts your eyes – so that's why they all wear shades?

author but could never be the work of just one person. So boundless thanks are due to many individuals and organisations whose assistance in its compilation has been invaluable. A whole posse of Harley riders and fans in America and Europe have helped and urged me on in all kinds of ways, supplying information, images and general bonhomie.

I'd especially like to single out Joe Schmidt of St James, Minnesota; Philip Tooth at *The Classic Motorcycle* for allowing me access to the magazine's archive; Sean Warwick and John Noble, editor and chief photographer of *Motor Cycle News* for similar duties; Louise Limb and Myatt McFarlane Publishing for some fine engine illustrations; Mick Woollett for library material; and ace photographers Mac McDiarmid and David Goldman for supplementing my own pictures.

Above
Such is the massive torque of the 1340cc Evolution engine that it virtually ignores all gradients (Mac McDiarmid)

Right
Everything, but everything for your Harley is for sale at Sturgis. Panhead, Shovelhead or Evolution owner, you could transplant a new heart into your motorcycle if you wished

Above

Attitude matters more than age when it comes to Electra Glide pilots and passengers

Left

With a longer wheelbase and long dualseat, pilot and passenger can stretch out on a modern Electra Glide

Above

Lights blazing and tassels tossing in the breeze, an FLH wafts its pilot along without a care in the world. Duo Glide FL and FLH models were not exactly fomenting a revolution in motorcycle design when they were fitted with electric starting in 1965: most Japanese machines had gone electric, some as early as 1960

Right

This is what two-wheel touring is all about – the sense of being out there in a vast landscape (Mac McDiarmid)

Above

A trio of Glide pilots joins in the two-wheeled street theatre that's part of Daytona Beach's Bike Week – the start of the riding season. If it's March, it must be Daytona; if it's August it must be Sturgis

Left

Dresser shows inevitably draw large crowds of admiring onlookers

Above

The 'solid' front wheel look, pioneered by Harley's Fat Boy, makes a rare appearance on an Electra Glide

Right

The Electra Glide glues itself to the highway and stays on line, allowing the rider and passenger to converse or just gawk at the scenery

Above
Swapping the seat material for something even more comfortable and attractive is a favourite ploy for FL owners

Left
Where the heck does this dust come from? An entrant at the dresser show applies more elbow grease before the judging commences

Above

To pamper the passenger, Ultra versions of the Classic FLH feature a separate pair of rear speakers with their own controls

Left

Life's a beach at Daytona. The Harley-Davidson record in competition on the sands is a fascinating reflection of how well or badly the company was perfoming as a whole – whether it be battling with the Manx Nortons in the 1950s, or losing out to the Japanese in the 1970s

Above
*Belonging to the Harley Owners Group
has become a way of life for some
enthusiasts*

Left
*Dangerous Don scans the waves from
the vantage point of his 1975 FLH*

Overleaf
*A couple of Glides coast down a
Wyoming road towards Devil's Tower
– the famous location from the
Spielberg film 'Close Encounters of the
Third Kind'*

Origins

It's extraordinary to think that of over 300 manufacturers that were established in the United States of America since motorised cycles were first dreamed up, just two survived to see action in the Second World War. With the demise of Indian in 1953, Harley-Davidson became the sole survivor of an industry that had witnessed such enormous variety and innovation, yet had succumbed so disastrously to financial and market forces. No wonder they called it The Great Depression.

The reasons why Harley-Davidson was able to keep going while others fell by the wayside aren't easy to quantify, but must have something to do with the machines' quality and durability. Other probable factors were the

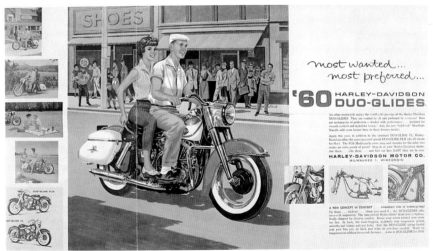

Above

Advertising for the 1960 Duo-Glide led on the bike's smooth suspension and good looks. Much was made of the bike's bold new appearance, with its distinctive headlight nacelle and natty Twin-Flare two-tone paint scheme. Two versions were offered – the standard FL and the special FLH, with H standing for 'hot'

Left

The first Harley-Davidson with hydraulic suspension at both front and rear was the Duo-Glide, launched in 1958. Soon it was to become the Electra Glide's daddy

sheer determination of the makers, the strength of its dealer network and the never ending loyalty of its customer base. Even with the benefit of hindsight the picture remains unclear, but we must be grateful that Harley pulled through. A product that looks, sounds and works as good as their characteristic V-twin deserves to live on.

Because Harley-Davidson has always been a cautious manufacturer, with a deliberate – some might prefer the word slow – rate of development, the American 'King of the Road' of the mid-60s didn't hatch overnight. Any bike wearing Harley's eagle badge doesn't spring from a clean sheet – it's invariably the result of years of thoughtful, careful and meticulously conscientious development. No-one can ever accuse Harley-Davidson of

Above

Electra Glide – the most evocative name in motorcycling bar none. The two flowing words of this metal badge have upped the heartbeat for three decades and show no sign of losing their grip on the two-wheeled psyche

Right

Anyone with a 1965 Electra Glide – the first year of production – owns a piece of American folklore. In the state of Minnesota, Joe Schmidt is steadily renovating this superb example and it should be back on the road by the time this book is published. While tearing down the engine he's even taken the trouble to repaint the frame and parts in the correct references – holiday red and birch white. What does he ride in the meantime? Another Electra Glide naturally, this time an '87 model

Elvis Presley's
1976
HARLEY DAVIDSON 1200

Has Been on Tour in....
N.Y. N.J. MD. PENN.& TENN.

Elvis Presley's Homes

BEVERLY
HILLS
144 MONOVALE

PALM SPRINGS
845 CHINO
CANYON RD.

IS CYCLE
INSURED BY LLOYDS
OF LONDON
CURRENTLY TITLED TO
ELVIS A.PRESLEY

Above

Once you've realised the dream and acquired your Electra Glide, what comes next? You customise it, of course, though some riders go further than others with this very public art form. Don't ask what it costs to create something like this beauty, because there's far more than substantial amounts of money involved. And once you start, where the heck do you stop?

Left

There are many who believe that the Almighty rode an Electra Glide and while we can't confirm that, we know the King certainly did! Elvis's 1976 FLH 1200 is on display at the Pioneer Auto Museum in Murdo, South Dakota

rushing headlong into innovation, that's for sure.

The manner in which Harley builds and develops its motorcycles is also unique because most 'modern' Harleys are in reality hybrids. Rather than creating new bikes completely from scratch, the company usually takes the best and most successful elements from one machine and integrates them into another. This method makes for a distinctly different as opposed to a new motorcycle – it's what constitutes 'new' for most Harleys. For these reasons it's essential to look back at the Electra Glide's lineage, to see how its predecessors shaped this most famous of tourers.

A new era of two-wheeled transportation was ushered into existence in Milwaukee by a young 20 year old pattern maker named Arthur Davidson and his 21 year old boyhood friend William S Harley who worked as a draughtsman at the same company. Both enjoyed toying with design ideas, and soon two of Arthur's brothers, Walter and William were helping along

Above

In lighter colours or gleaming white, later versions of the Electra Glide show that unmistakable profile that can't help but turn heads on the street

Left

When your butt is in the saddle all day the ride had better be comfortable or else. That's why many US patrolmen choose a pared down version of the Electra Glide, the FLHP, for their daily duties. Come the weekend many of these guys then hop on their own Harleys – is that what they call going the whole hog?

with what was in the first place not much more than a hobby.

Actually, the fledgling Harley-Davidson company's first motorcycle in 1903, produced in a 10x15 foot wooden shed in the back garden, was a single cylinder machine of just 161cc or 10 cubic inches. Legend has it that the carburettor was a modified tomato can and the machine was named the 'Silent Grey Fellow' to reflect the company's desire to keep motorcycling a quiet pastime. A later, enlarged version pumped out a mere 3 horses, so its pedals were often needed to enhance forward motion. A search for greater power led to experiments with twin-cylinder engines and 1909 saw the first 'real' Harley – a 45° V-twin design that has become synonymous with the marque. This one displaced 1000cc or 61 cu in and its seven hp could bowl it along at 60mph.

As early as 1922, Harley-Davidson had produced a huge 1200cc/74 cu in V-twin engine, though the first overhead valve design didn't come along until 1936 in the shape of the 61E. The 'Knucklehead' engine had a capacity of 1000cc/61cu in and delivered double the power of the older 61 design. Even more output was available with the enlarged capacity 1200cc/74 cu in version of 1941, but the American public had little time to sample its urge as Harley's total production was diverted to the war effort shortly afterwards.

These were black years for Harley-Davidson for other reasons too. The late 1930s and early 1940s witnessed the deaths of three of the company's founding quartet – William A Davidson in 1937, Walter Davidson in 1942 and William S Harley a year later. When Arthur Davidson died in a car crash in 1950, all four had perished and the company passed totally to a new generation of managers to maintain the family's proud tradition.

Civilian machines began rolling off the assembly lines once more in 1947, and Harley were able to offer improvements to the hot 74 incher glimpsed at the start of that decade. A move typical of the company's linear evolution was seen in 1948 with the introduction of the 'new' Panhead V-twin. Of course 'new' meant that this was in fact a Knucklehead with a fresh top end and a revised lubrication system, but progress is progress however it's couched.

Offered in both 1000cc/61 cu in and 1200cc/74 cu in capacities, the Panhead – so called because its rocker covers were shaped like baking pans – featured novel hydraulic valve lifters. At first they were fitted towards the top of the engine between the pushrods and the rocker arm, but this system proved troublesome so they were moved to their now familiar location between the cam lobe and the pushrod inside the timing case.

Right
Daytona Beach in early March, then Sturgis in August are the two major pilgrimages on the American rally calendar for Harley-Davidson riders

Above

Any gathering of Harleys isn't complete without a dresser show. If you were under the impression that Electra Glides were the least customised machines out of Milwaukee, attending one of these events soon puts you right

Left

This is what all the fuss was about – the redundancy of the Harley's kickstarter. First versions of the Electra Glide in 1965 were powered by the Panhead motor that had seen sterling service from soon after the Second World War. Sadly the electric starter wasn't all that great at cranking the engine over in humid conditions

But the new top end cured the problem of oil control and excessive consumption, its internal oilways minimising oil leaks. With its aluminium cylinder heads the Panhead powered Harley through to the middle of the 1960s. The 61 cu in E designated engine was discontinued in 1954 leaving just the larger F versions – F for standard and FL for higher compression. Soon the latter engine became the standard, and a much modified, although similar-looking, bottom end was also introduced in 1955.

Alongside these engine changes, things were also happening to the Harley's cycle parts. In 1949 the factory finally abandoned the springer front suspension design of the big twin (though it was to return in the 1980s in a fit of nostalgia styling) and opted instead for a simpler telescopic fork design. This suspension system used helical springs inside tubes which were hydraulically dampened with oil. The telescopic method afforded greater wheel travel enabling softer springs and a superior ride quality.

Here also were the beginnings of the naming and styling of the modern V-twin range, with this particular stab at modernity labelled the Hydra-Glide. The first half of the hyphenated name referring to the hydraulic action of the new front fork, and the second part that it glided down the road. Or perhaps Harley simply used the word because it sounded right.

The Hydra-Glide also had a new look about it, symptomatic of the age. Its chunky tyres were adorned with fully valanced fenders, and those telescopic forks up front were shrouded with covers, topped with a nacelle for the headlamp. Soon afterwards the controls were offered with the modern layout of hand-operated clutch and a foot shifter for the gears – but not everyone liked it! The weight of the bike hovered around 600 lbs, but it could just reach over the magic three figures out on the highway given a long enough straight, and there were plenty of those around.

In the '50s riders had started to kit out their FLs with touring gear – windshields made of canvas, plus leather saddlebags. These were supplied by both Harley and a few outside companies, and enabled a rider to sit comfortably upright and not get blown right off the machine as speeds crept beyond 60mph.

These customised 'dressers' obviously caught the factory's eye too, eventually leading to the first stock dressed machine in 1966. Until then riders made their own FLH 'King of the Highway' by installing a clear windshield and leather saddlebags, to keeping most of the bugs and breeze from the rider's torso and provide some luggage space for his belongings. Quite how far he'd want to ride with that rigid rear end was a matter for some conjecture, though many hard butts managed trips across several states without batting an eyelid. Greater comfort was just around the corner, however.

Some ten years after they'd sorted out the front end of the big V-twin, Harley got round to looking at the back. For 1958 they placed a pair of chrome-shrouded springs there and changed the bike's title to Duo-Glide. Like the Hydra-Glide, this sounded good and effectively described the changes they'd made – springs at both ends of the bike. The name also looked fabulous as a wire badge on the side of the front fender.

Above right
A tank-mounted speedo as big as an alarm clock and fillers on each of the dual tanks were Electra Glide trademarks right through until the 1980s

Below right
A typical dude at an H-D rally, with obligatory beard and shades. ZZ Top have a lot to answer for

Opposite
Leading link or 'springer' forks were finally abandoned by Harley-Davidson in the late '40s in favour of the telescopic fork. The improved ride this gave led to the first use of the word 'glide', with the Hydra-Glide model of 1949

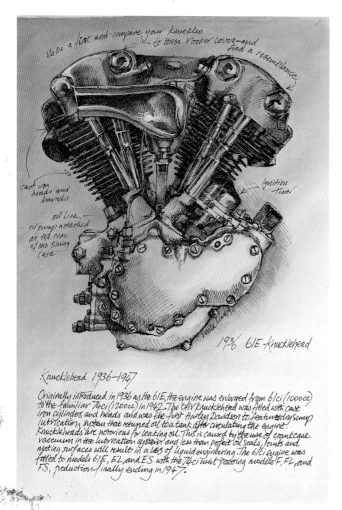

Make a fist and compare your knuckles to these 'rocker' covers – and find a resemblance

cast iron heads and barrels

Ignition timer

oil line – oil pump attached at the rear of the timing case

1936 61E – Knucklehead

Knucklehead 1936–1947

Originally introduced in 1936 as the 61E, the engine was enlarged from 61ci (1000cc) to the familiar 74ci (1200cc) in 1942. The OHV Knucklehead was fitted with cast iron cylinders and heads and was the first Harley Davidson to feature a dry sump lubrication system that returned oil to a tank after circulating the engine. Knuckleheads are notorious for leaking oil. This is caused by the use of crankcase vacuum in the lubrication system and less than perfect oil seals, joints and mating surfaces will result in a loss of liquid engineering. The 61ci engine was fitted to models 61E, EL, and ES with the 74ci unit powering models F, FL, and FS, production finally ending in 1947.

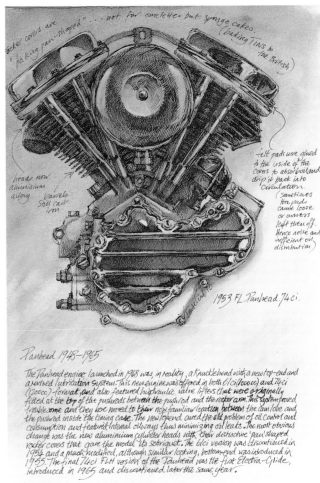

rocker covers are 'pan-shaped'... not for omelettes but sponge cakes (baking tins to the British)

heads now aluminium alloy

barrels still cast iron

felt pads were glued to the inside of the covers to absorb oil and drip it back into circulation. (sometimes the pads came loose or owners left them off. Hence noise and inefficient oil distribution)

1953 FL Panhead 74ci.

Panhead 1948–1965

The Panhead engine launched in 1948 was, in reality, a Knucklehead with a new top-end and a revised lubrication system. This new engine was offered in both 61ci (1000cc) and 74ci (1200cc) format, and also featured hydraulic valve lifters that were originally fitted at the top of the pushrods between the pushrod and the rocker arm. This system proved troublesome and they were moved to their now familiar location between the cam lobe and the pushrod inside the timing case. The new top-end cured the old problem of oil control and consumption and featured internal oilways thus minimizing oil leaks. The most obvious change was the new aluminium cylinder heads with their distinctive 'pan-shaped' rocker covers that gave the model its sobriquet. The 61ci version was discontinued in 1954 and a much modified, although similar looking, bottom-end was introduced in 1955. The final 74ci FLH version of the Panhead was the first Electra-Glide, introduced in 1965 and discontinued later the same year.

Introduced in 1936, the Knucklehead ohv V-twin originally had a capacity of 1000cc/61 cu in but grew to the familiar 1200cc/74 cu in by 1942. This was the first Harley to feature dry sump lubrication that returned oil to a tank after circulating the engine. The last engines were made in 1947, heralding the Panhead era

In reality, the new Panhead of 1948 was a Knucklehead with a new top end and a revised lubrication system. It was offered in 1000cc/61 cu in and 1200cc/74 cu in formats, and featured hydraulic valve lifters. The aluminium heads had distinctive 'pan-shaped' rocker covers that led to the engine's nickname. The final Panheads appeared in 1965 coinciding with the launch of the Electra Glide

The first Harley-Davidson 'factory' in 1903 was a 15x10 feet wooden shed built by cabinet maker William C Davidson, father of the founding brothers. It was sited in the Davidson family home's back yard in Milwaukee (Harley-Davidson photo)

To cater for the new, large fibreglass saddlebags at the back, Harley had to position the rear suspension units too close to the swinging arm pivot, and this adversely affecting the handling. This was just one of the compromises the big twins carried along with them into the 1960s.

Starting up the vast 1200cc/74 cu in mill was something of an art in itself – much mystique had been generated about the proper techniques needed. Even with an engine in good tune, sometimes the thing wouldn't spring to life even after two or three hearty swings on the kickstarter. Tall, muscular dudes had the brawn to cope with repeated kicks, but for smaller, skinnier types the thought of expending loads of energy just to fire her up was a daunting prospect, especially on a nippy winter's morning. Something had to be done, but it wouldn't be reality until the middle of the 1960s – the start of the Electra Glide era.

Above left

Four men sharing a desire to take the effort out of cycling were the founders of a motorcycle legend – from the left William A Davidson, Walter Davidson, Arthur Davidson and William S Harley (Harley-Davidson photo)

Left

A lifestyle packed with outdoor adventure, or at least hot coffee, was promised if you bought into the dream and obtained a Duo-Glide. This is a 1964 bike, dressed with windshield and saddlebags (Harley-Davidson photo)

Above

After thirty years the wheel has turned full circle for the Electra Glide, with the debut of the 'undressed' FLHR Road King (John Noble/MCN)

What's In A Name?

After labelling their first motorcycle the 'Silent Grey Fellow', Harley-Davidson fell into the habit of identifying their products by anonymous letters or numbers for the next half century. Naturally owners gave their bikes, and even engines, nicknames to make them cosier but all that changed in 1949, when the Hydra-Glide first saw the light of day. Nearly a decade later its successor – the Duo-Glide – entered production. By the same token the K model turned into the Sportster in the '50s – another durable if highly modified Harley design spanning across the years.

So names were in and that chosen for the new tourer for 1965, boosted by luxuries like a 12 volt electric system and a push-button starter was, quite naturally, Electra-Glide. Again Harley had got it spot on, creating, to many, the best sounding name ever to adorn a motorcycle. Like its parents, the two words were at first joined by a hyphen. Later the hyphen was quietly dropped.

The centre section of the Duo-Glide's frame had been opened up slightly to allow for the starter motor. This was mounted aft of the cylinders, where it could crank the engine through the primary drive. There was also space for a beefier battery. This 12 volt 32 aH was deemed sufficient to crank the motor into life on cold mornings, and provide ample power for the large sealed-beam headlight, taillight and direction indicators. A casualty of all this was the toolbox, for which there was no room anymore

Sadly, the outside contractor messed up the first batch of starters, which functioned admirably providing there wasn't a drop of moisture in the atmosphere. This was slightly ironic as the design was first applied to outboard motors on boats! Fortunately Harley left the kick-starter on to reassure those who didn't fancy bump starting such a hefty bike. With the company covered in embarrassment, the starter was soon changed for a version manufactured by Homelite, and this one functioned efficiently. It must have done the job fine because by 1970 the kickstart lever had been deleted.

Of course, there was no way the new Electra Glide could have a new motor too – it had to share the same old big, booming, air-cooled V-twin, then of 1200cc or 74 cubic inches, as the rest of the range. The new bike adhered to the V-twin tradition for all kinds of reasons. Its compact design packs the largest capacity into the narrowest width, so frontal area is minimised. The V could also be slung low in the frame to give a lower

Gleaming chrome and polished aluminium everywhere – this 1965 Panhead Electra Glide probably wasn't as immaculate as this when it came off the production line thirty years ago. Note the serrated cover protecting the front exhaust pipe

This painstakingly restored '65 Electra Glide is close to the original specification apart from curious curved metalwork on the front fender and the spring assists under the seat. Its owner purchased it as a 'basket case' and set to work, completing the project in 1990

centre of gravity, better stability and a reasonable seat height. This layout also combined simplicity with plenty of power along with excellent fuel efficiency.

Just one easily adjusted carburettor was needed between the cylinders, enabling the engine to produce a wide band of power with lots of torque lower down the rev range where it was most useful. The uncomplicated nature of the V-twin meant it had excellent durability and reliability, and could be easily maintained. Given these virtues, there's little wonder the V-twin has become a Harley trademark.

One engine design quirk that passed down the years is the fact that the huge cylinders sit directly one behind the other along the frame's longitudinal axis. A forked conrod is used to connect the crankshaft to the rear piston, while the rod for the front piston nestles inside it on the crankpin. Neat though this layout is, the point has often been raised that

A dualseat and fishtail mufflers are among the accessories added to this 1965 Electra Glide seen in South Dakota. Apart from the electric starter, it is really very little different from its Duo-Glide ancestor

offsetting the cylinders slightly would permit the rear barrel to receive greater cooling as the bike moves forward through the airstream. The realignment has never taken place, and as the rearmost cylinder naturally runs hotter than the forward one, a cooler heat range spark plug is often fitted there for added safety.

Having touched upon the V-twins dependability, no engine can be perfect. The Panhead mill was once described as being 'as reliable as the path of the sun', but owners' testimony appears to paint a different picture. Several examples of main bearing were reported, and the motor also exhibited a healthy appetite for chains, neither of which was good news unless you enjoyed wielding a serious number of spanners.

The standard gearbox fitted was a four speeder, though right through until 1980 you could also order a version from the factory with three forward speeds and a reverse gear. This was for sidecar use, of course. Of a

Above
The proportions of the 1200cc Electra Glide may have seemed daunting in the 1960s, but the same bike appears quite compact compared to some of its modern counterparts

Right
Single seat is held aloft on a column rising from the main frame, much like a bicycle. Note the massive battery box

Left

The generously valanced mudguards or fenders were part of a styling package that came in during the late 1940s. Look at some '90s machines and there's very little difference

Above

The 'buddy' seat enabled an Electra Glide pilot to take along a passenger too, as long as they were good friends! A longer wheelbase was several years off when this Electra Glide was made

build quality that wouldn't look out of place in a truck, the gearbox makes up in strength what it lacks in silence. On any Electra Glide including the first ones, gear lever travel is extensive, and changing cogs is more often than not accompanied by a loud clank from the transmission. The challenge to make that noiseless shift is something all 'Glide owners aspire to, but rarely achieve.

For years the bigger Harley-Davidson's had featured flat footboards for the riders feet, while the rest of the motorcycle world contented itself with round pegs. These were carried over onto the Electra Glide, and, because of their broad area, were comfortable for a range of owners. They also allowed shifts to different positions, but one drawback was that significant engine vibration and wind pressure combined to slide the foot back from its intended spot. H-D had its head in the sand about the small matter of engine vibration – after all, didn't all real bikes do that?

The 1965 Electra Glide may have shook, but it sure looked a picture. Those 5 inch whitewall tyres on spoked wheels really set off the two-tone paint scheme, and the proportions of the machine just could not have been bettered. However, as already observed, Harley had put form before function in the matter of the rear suspension units.

Law enforcement riders – a substantial market for the Milwaukee factory – needed room for their emergency kit back there and most ordinary buyers wanted the handy panniers. Placing the suspension too close to the swinging arm pivot gave the big twin some peculiar handling characteristics while turning corners, and meant it hardly fell into the nimble category. And yet somehow, provided you didn't press the bike, the Electra Glide negotiated turns in its own majestic fashion.

Carrying far more equipment than the earlier plain Hydra-Glide, a 1965 FLH tipped the scales at over 780 lbs. Top speed had dipped to just under

After just a year with the Panhead engine, the Electra Glide moved on to the Shovelhead for '66. Despite the luxury of an electric start, the kick starter remained on the bike for a few years, just in case

Harley's brochure for the 1966 Electra Glide made great noises about the Shovelhead's extra urge. Five more horses were available at the twist of a wrist for enhanced acceleration and cruising, but the horrible drum brakes weren't too effective at hauling the beast to a halt

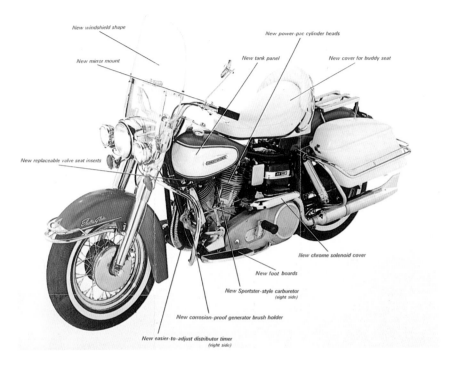

fast action and smooth with big horsepower build-up for '66

New windshield shape
New mirror mount
New replaceable valve seat inserts
New power-pac cylinder heads
New tank panel
New cover for buddy seat
New chrome solenoid cover
New foot boards
New Sportster-style carburetor *(right side)*
New corrosion-proof generator brush holder
New easier-to-adjust distributor timer *(right side)*

100mph and the drum brakes were given a hard time stopping all that mass in motion. After decades as a reasonably trim motorcycle, the new tourer had turned into a true heavyweight.

1965 witnessed the launch of the Electra Glide, and it was also the year when the privately held Harley-Davidson corporation went public. Short of capital and increasingly aware of the ominously growing influx of imported motorcycles, shares were offered for general sale.

The venerable Panhead V-twin had seen trojan service from shortly after the Second World War right through into the mid-1960s, but it lasted just one model year in the Electra Glide. For 1966, Harley-Davidson slotted in their new Shovelhead mill, again of 1200cc/74 cu in. An advert for the bike, pictured blasting away in front of hordes of galloping horses, claimed it was 10% more powerful than the '65, and boasted of its new styling finesse and enhanced comfort features.

In truth, the Shovelhead followed familiar Harley engine practice, by adding a new top-end to the tried and tested bottom half of the Panhead. The new power-pac aluminium cylinder heads featured bolt-on cast alloy rocker boxes, and these were said by some to resemble the back of a coal

Above

Not recommended for emergency stops! The rear brake pedal has never been one of the Electra Glide's best features, and this one on a '67 model is positioned at a ridiculous angle. The truck-like brake pedal isn't a great aid to safety, as the foot has to be lifted away from the floorboard. All this takes up valuable milliseconds of braking time, so Harley pilots riding in traffic are, understandably, wont to ride with bags of anticipation

Left

Without saddlebags, the poor positioning of the suspension units on the swinging arm is all too obvious. They'd stay at this mechanical disadvantage until the early '80s

Left

Fishtail silencers and ornate fender brackets add a real styling flourish to the rear end

Above

Out for an evening run, this pristine 'generator' Shovelhead reverberates through these Florida trees – sheer music for rider, passenger and observer

shovel, hence the agreeable nickname 'Shovelhead'.

Cylinder barrels continued to be made of iron, which meant the retention of the hydraulic lifters was most necessary. The tall shape of the barrels meant a high rate of expansion and contraction, but the hydraulic system kept valve lash to zero and reduced the mechanical thrashing. There might also have been a problem where the iron barrels met the alloy crankcases, as they have different coefficients of expansion, but external oil lines prevented seepage from this area.

The Shovelhead engine remained unchanged for just four years. In 1970 new crankcases were introduced, eliminating the generator and replacing it with a crankshaft mounted alternator. There was also a clear cone-shape to the timing cover, which housed a contact breaker ignition system. Not surprisingly, the earlier engine was known as the Generator Shovel and the later design became the Alternator Shovel.

Harley's 1970 version of the Electra Glide was hardly state-of-the-art. However with its top box and saddlebags, more baggage could be carried than any other bike of its era, albeit slowly

From 1970 onward Shovelheads dropped the generator and replaced it with a crankshaft-mounted alternator. The contact breaker lived behind a cone-shaped cover, here adorned with the ubiquitous Harley eagle

For the first few years of production the Electra Glide had the option of a police-style handlebar-mounted windshield. Made of vinyl, they were available in a clear finish or with a red or blue coloured panel at the base. The bag, also from the accessory catalogue, kept maps, gloves or glasses handy

The switch of engine was the major event for the Electra Glide models of the late 1960s, as in true Harley fashion the rest of the motorcycle was just tinkered with here and there. For the 1967 model year, the big Harley tourer saw only minor refinements, such as a mildly reshaped intake port and the attachment of a Tillotson diaphragm carburettor. The beauty of the latter was that it could be tuned without removal – the previous carb had to be detached to change its jets.

With an average-sized rider aboard and some luggage, the all-up weight of the Electra Glide wasn't much shy of 1000 lbs, placing even greater strain on its brakes. According to a *Cycle World* road test at the time, the stopping power of the 1967 model left something to be desired.

'In one very important area – brakes – the Electra Glide is terrible. The hydraulic rear brake is not bad, by itself. But it shouldn't have to work by itself, which in practice it does. The mechanical front brake has been around since 1949 and is most certainly due for retirement. As a hill-holder it is fine, but as a front brake for a heavy, fast motorcycle, it's laughable.'

In an era of largely uncritical reporting, such comments must have hurt the top-brass at the factory, but Harley-Davidson has never been panicked by criticism, no matter how influential the magazine. So the inefficient drum stopper remained on the front wheel for several years to come.

Early 'dresser' Electra Glides were fitted with a clear, police-type screen and spotlights up front. Only in 1969 was the large, half-painted fibreglass screen attached to the handlebars offered as an option. It's no coincidence that Harley-Davidson had acquired a fibreglass factory that same year. Unfashionably curvaceous in its day, it's little changed now and still looks utterly fabulous – perhaps the best fairing ever to be attached to any motorcycle, period.

For riders who wanted to travel with all their possessions on board, the full touring option included the fibreglass fairing, a Pak-King or pair of fibreglass saddlebags plus a third case placed high on a rack above the fender. Harley called it the Tour-Pak, though everyone else referred to it as a top box. There was also a standing joke about Harleys of the late 1960s being available with another optional accessory – a basket under the engine to catch parts as they fell off!

The sale of shares in Harley-Davidson in the middle of the 1960s had failed to generate sufficient cash to keep the company ahead of the pack – the Japanese manufacturers were more modern, more adept and more in tune with an increasingly sophisticated motorcycle-buying public. In 1969 further writing on the wall appeared in the shape of the Honda CB750 – Japan's first large-capacity sports tourer rival. It was announced the same year by Harley-Davidson that the company had merged with the conglomerate American Machine & Foundry (or AMF), though a more

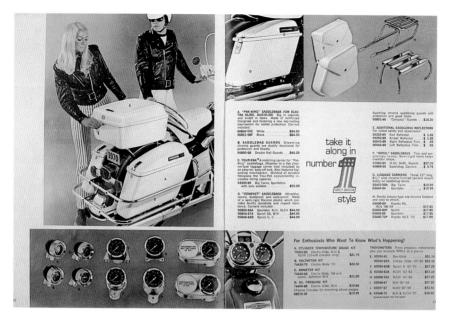

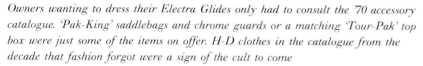

Owners wanting to dress their Electra Glides only had to consult the '70 accessory catalogue. 'Pak-King' saddlebags and chrome guards or a matching 'Tour-Pak' top box were just some of the items on offer. H-D clothes in the catalogue from the decade that fashion forgot were a sign of the cult to come

accurate term might have been swallowed up.

AMF were able to pump much-needed finances and resources into Harley-Davidson, but many saw the move as a retrograde step for the motorcycle manufacturer and a significant step in their decline. Without AMF, of course, the Milwaukee company would not have been able to keep up with product demand, as the 1970s were boom years for two wheelers in America.

In the latter half of the '60s, Harley's annual output had been averaging 25-30,000 bikes. By 1975, at the peak of the boom, the figure had jumped to 75,000 machines. Sadly the huge increase in volume was not matched in the area of quality control, and tales of flies embedded in paint and assorted mechanical horrors are legion. The Japanese motorcycle invasion of America had certainly wounded Harley-Davidson, but it hadn't eaten away at the special corner of the market the home-based manufacturer had created for itself.

Right

Now in his 70s, Neil from Kelso in Washington state has been riding his 1970 Electra Glide the 1400 miles to the Black Hills rally in Sturgis for many years. He's been owned by the bike for almost a quarter of a century and despite 200,000 miles on the clock it's never let him down. A rebuild at 168,000 is the only work that's been needed. Would he swap his old friend for a more modern Glide? Don't ask silly questions

Above

The police-type screen gave the Electra Glide pilot a clear view of the road ahead but offered a useful degree of protection from the elements (MCN)

Left

While Honda were wheeling out their modern CB750 four-cylinder sports machine in 1970, showing a glimpse of what was to come, Harley persevered with their elderly but simple V-twin

Above

What a way to treat an Electra Glide, with countless chrome lights all over it. The owners seem quite happy with their creation, though (MCN)

Right

Chrome saddlebag guards avoided damaging the fibreglass and also looked the part. Shame the lids tended to fly off unless they were securely locked. Fibreglass was always going to feature on H-D machinery, not just because it was a wonderful substance, but also because the company bought into fibreglass technology in the AMF era by buying a suitably knowledgable subsidiary

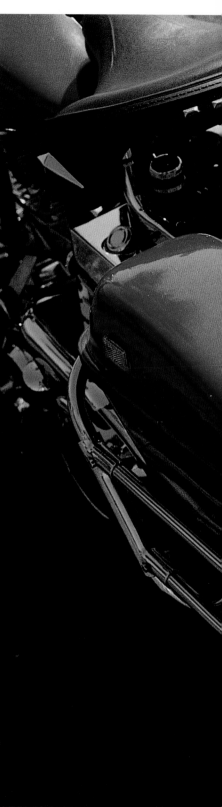

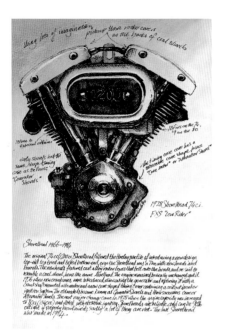

Above

First seen on the Electra Glide in 1966, the 1200cc/74 cu in Shovelhead followed the Harley practice of introducing a new top end to a tried and tested bottom half. New crankcases followed in 1970, featuring this cone-shaped timing cover and replacing the generator with an alternator. In 1978 the engine was bored out to 1340cc/80 cu in and fitted with electronic ignition

Right

The addition of an alternator to Shovelheads from 1970 on meant the engine was even wider and this pushed the floorboards out, further limiting cornering ability

Mid-life Crisis

Continuing serenely on its way through the 1970s, the Electra Glide looked and performed much as it had done during the '60s, and not much different from its big twin predecessors of the '50s for that matter. Japanese sports bikes, often employing a fraction of the engine capacity, had long left the big tourer for dead in the performance stakes, but in Milwaukee that was missing the point.

Not for Harley-Davidson the sweeping changes and staccato frenzy of a new model introduction every other year. Their concerns were still about slow evolvement and gradually improving quality, though at times during the decade you'd have been hard pressed to find the latter theory translated into metal.

One improvement was there for all to see, however. To answer widespread criticism about its braking abilities, or lack of them, the Electra Glide at last acquired a hydraulic disc front brake in 1972. The single caliper unit was certainly neatly designed, and had the writers of the time drooling over its merits. 'Super-powerful, its performance dwarfs that of the earlier drum' wrote *Motorcycle Sport Quarterly*, revealing how

Above right
Apart from the addition of the fibreglass fairing, there was little to distinguish the FLH1200's of the '70s from the '60s. This is a '73 model (Harley-Davidson photo)

Right
Because the exhaust pipes overhung several inches behind the rear wheel, they were often scraped while riding over kerbs or even during parking. Disc brakes arrived up front in 1972, and this '74 model had a Keihin carburettor but otherwise only cosmetic changes (Harley-Davidson photo)

Left
The years when AMF held sway at Harley-Davidson are often regarded as one of the company's low points in their cycles of fortune. Quality control suffered as production leapt to keep up with the boom's demand for motorcycles. The heel and toe shift levers soon become familiar but limit the size of a pilot's boot

Because the Electra Glide has changed so little and so slowly, it's quite common to find a bike with parts from different years all bolted together. This machine from the AMF era has post-'72 disc brakes front and rear, but a pre-'70 gearbox complete with kickstarter. Note the Number 1 stars and stripes logo on the timing cover, to commemorate Harley's competition successes of 1969

the writers of the period were grateful for even small mercies.

Despite the innovative tag the Japanese invaders had commandeered, the Electra Glide was the first motorcycle in the world to feature full hydraulic braking both front and rear, but it still took a lot of effort at the handlebar to persuade it to shed speed. Another innovation for '72 was self-cancelling indicators.

Vibration was the dominant impression given by the '73 model, but you could have picked any year of this period and found the same result. A softly padded buddy seat and rubber-mounted handlebars shielded the rider from some shakes, but the excessive vibes transmitted through the flat footboards meant it was hard to keep your feet on the motorcycle at highway cruising speeds.

Straight line handling was steady as a rock, but any sweeping curves had to be attempted with a modicum of sense – the low-hanging footboards would send up a shower of sparks otherwise. It must be said

Above

To answer criticisms of the 'Buddy' seat, Harley featured a longer and lower perch for 1977, labelled the Comfort Flex. This placed the passenger higher than the pilot for a better view

Right

A large backrest has been added for the passenger's benefit on this '77 FLH 1200. Polished panels also tidy up the bike ahead of the saddlebag area

the big tourer wasn't set up for blasting from corner to corner, as its weight and soft suspension settings precluded any such style of riding. But riders who pointed the beast at the horizon found the Harley would do their bidding all day.

With production running at ever higher levels, space in the Milwaukee factory was at a premium and the quality of workmanship and finish of the bikes was suffering. AMF owned a large factory in York, Pennsylvania, but a move there away from Harley's home in Milwaukee was deemed politically sensitive. Nevertheless that's what happened in 1974, and the situation got a little ugly. The facility was far superior to anything Harley had used before, with a vast and efficient overhead conveyor system installed. But there were reports of sabotage by disgruntled workers, and plenty of bad feelings going around. AMF were portrayed as an insensitive conglomerate, with dubious intentions for the famous old motorcycle firm they'd taken over.

In truth the bad press AMF suffered around this time seems hardly justified now. Mistakes were certainly made but the parent company ploughed millions of dollars into H-D, improving the production facilities out of sight and possibly even saving the company from oblivion. In hindsight three factors all occurring around the mid-'70s seem to have put the skids under their relationship. First, the almost threefold increase in output, coupled with a wider and more complicated model range. Second, the waning of the motorcycle boom meant that demand was slipping. And the third factor was the imported Gold Wing. What Harley were about to discover was that the rules of the touring world were about to change, forever. Honda had got serious and launched a large, 1000cc touring bike built in Japan, but tailored to American tastes. Here at last was a real touring rival for the Electra Glide – a modern machine which carried all kinds of threatening signals for Harley-Davidson.

Having had the market to themselves for so long, H-D wasn't well placed or even inclined to respond immediately. So the latter part of the '70s saw the Electra Glide continuing to plough its furrow, notable only for the fitting of one or two parts sourced from Japan. So much for the all-American motorcycle, but don't mention that within earshot of any dyed-in-the-wool Harley fan, unless you fancy an argument. In 1977 the buddy seat bowed out, replaced by a longer, lower double-bucket Comfort Flex perch.

The King of the Road remained a massive, heavy and cumbersome bike, and still exhibited a tendency to spin-in while pootling along slowly. Out on the open road was another matter, 'cos the 'Glide was in its element. Cruising lazily along somewhere near the speed limit, the giant bore and stroke of the motor produced a satisfyingly relaxed exhaust rhythm and little in the way of noticeable vibration. Great slabs of torque meant

Above

To celebrate 75 years of motorcycle production, Harley-Davidson launched an anniversary special edition in 1978. The engine was the bored and stroked Shovelhead, now up to 1340cc/80 cu in, wearing a large new air cleaner. Attractive cast alloy wheels were also featured. If you can stay in manufacturing for ninety years, you have plenty of excuses for parties and special editions

Right

Harley-Davidson is fond of birthdays – theirs or anyone else's for that matter. The '70s saw a rash of motorcycles bearing commemorative cosmetics, including that for America's Bicentennial in 1976

Above

Though nearly two decades have passed since it came off the production line, this Colorado-based 1978 Limited Edition FLH has only covered 17000 miles and has a really proud second owner. Just 850 examples were produced

Right

This early version of the FLT Tour Glide with 1340cc Shovelhead engine shows how little the design has changed over the years since its 1980 debut. Another departure for Harley was the FLT's massive twin-headlamp layout – enough to light up any highway. That huge King-Pak and saddlebags would hold enough gear for weeks on the road

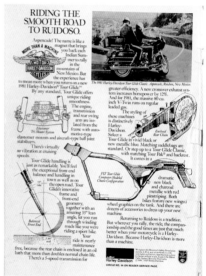

Above

Revamped frame geometry in the form of the FLT Tour Glide was seen in 1980, and Harley were still banging the drum about its technology a year later when this advert appeared. Elastomer engine mounts, 'balanced' front end, revised frame and enclosed rear drive at last meant that Harley were awakening from their slumbers. Another tradition started to ebb away as the FLT used a conventional single petrol tank with a central filler cap underneath a locking panel

headwinds and most gradients were simply ignored, and the bike remained as if on rails until bumpy bends or too great an angle of lean was attempted. All this and it returned 50mpg too, no matter how much stuff was carried.

For 1978 the capacity of the faithful Shovelhead motor was bored and stroked up to 1340cc/80cu in, and breathed through a huge new high-flow aircleaner. The smaller 1200cc/74 cu in engine continued to be available too. Under prodding by the EPA, Harley also fitted the FLH-80 with V-fire electronic ignition system made for them by Presto-Lite. The dreaded solid state black box had arrived, but die-hards still junked them in favour of a conventional points and condenser system. Then as now, black boxes are fine when they work and even give a slight increase in bhp. But when they go, they go, and there ain't no point in trying to fix 'em.

Stylish cast alloy wheels were also seen around this period on the 80 inchers, so traditional laced spokes were on their way out too. And the sprung seat appeared on its last legs, as for 1979 you could order a version of the FLH-80 with a saddle that was frame-mounted and gave a lower 28 inch seat height. Classic versions were fitted with all the goodies as standard including the TourPak and backrest. You could even choose

between three different sets of gear ratios!

Only in 1980, at the same time as Honda unveiled a new 1100cc Gold Wing, did Harley-Davidson bring out a motorcycle that revealed fresh thinking and a unity of design. The Tour Glide, or FLT, came with a wholly new frame and a first for Milwaukee – a five-speed gearbox. Almost every other manufacturer had been putting five cogs in their transmissions for years, but no matter.

Harley-Davidson's first really new model for over a decade was to have a major effect upon the existing Electra Glide, which continued in production alongside. The FLT used the same 80 cu in Shovelhead engine, 16in wheels, low seat and full dresser accessories but, importantly, it featured a drivetrain tailored to the new frame and suspension. It also sported a completely new, much larger fairing attached to the frame, with dual headlamps up front to light the way.

These new pieces wrapped around the traditional V-twin to represent

Above
With the Tour Glide's larger, frame-mounted fairing, legshields can be made a snugger fit than on the Electra Glide. Here they form a continuous surface to keep wind at bay and offer optimum protection, whereas the fork-mounted design needs substantial gaps to permit the bars to turn and not impede the fairing

Right
FLT Tour Glide among friends at Sturgis

Harley's belated entry into the modern motorcycling era. Engine vibrations were isolated by a series of soft rubber mounts that owed something to the British Norton's Isolastic design for the Commando – another large capacity twin. These flexible, biscuit-type rubber mounts allowed the engine/transmission/final drive assembly to move up and down or back and forth, but restricted lateral movement. The system didn't actually reduce vibration, but transmitted less to the rider which amounted to the same thing. It also meant the seat could be solidly mounted, and that the floorboards no longer had to be sprung.

Other firsts on the FLT were the fully-enclosed final drive chain in its own oil bath, and larger triple discs with a 12 inch unit at the rear and twin 10 inchers up front. The fairing was mounted to the frame but the instrument pod at the steering head turned with the handlebars – a significant move away from the tank-mounted pod of previous Harley tourers.

Above

Has the Tour Glide design been a benefit to the Electra Glide or not? Opinions vary but the FLT gets the thumbs up from this pilot. Note the backrest for added touring comfort (David Goldman)

Right

When you're watching dirt track racing, you won't find a more comfortable perch than the seat of your FLT

Most novel of all was the front-end geometry. With a steering head angle of 25° and fork tubes mounted behind the steering head, there would normally have been very little trail and the design would have proved unstable. But this Harley had the fork tubes offset 4° 15' from the steering head, giving almost 6 inches of trail – slightly more than with the conventional FLH frame and steering. This carefully crafted front end placed the centre of gravity behind the pivot point, giving a strong self-centring effect.

The new front end geometry enabled the Tour Glide to steer faster with just gentle pressure on the bars, and gave excellent balance and stability. To retain sufficient steering lock, the new frame placed the steering head far enough forward so that the forks would turn fully yet without colliding with the newly designed petrol tank. Other advantages of the frame were greater ground clearance – some 2 inches better than the

Above
Light but strong toothed-belt secondary drive to the rear wheel was introduced on the FLH Classic from 1983 onwards. Soon the FLHTC and the FLT Tour Glide got it too

Left
To answer the need for greater urge, Harley increased the displacement of the Shovelhead motor in 1978 up to 1340cc/80cu in. This is one of the last of its type from the mid-'80s before the Evolution engine made its bow

Left
Simplicity is the keynote to Harley's V-twin, and it can be torn down and worked on without fear or hesitation. This Shovelhead was receiving attention under cover at Sturgis. Servicing and maintenance while-u-wait was on offer – a good job as some of the bikes were ridden thousands of hard, hot miles to reach this mecca of motorcycling

Above
A 1978 Electra Glide undergoing road testing by a British motorcycling journal. The magazine has long passed away but Harley's grand tourer powers on (Mick Woollett)

contemporary Electra Glide – to permit greater cornering angles of lean. Some 35° of lean was claimed with the machine loaded.

Speaking of which the important statistic of load capacity had suddenly increased substantially. The 1980 Electra Glide weighed 722 lbs dry and could manage a load of 395 lbs, but the new Tour Glide weighing 725 lbs had the capacity to carry 455 lbs.

Nor had Harley forgotten a long-term design weakness towards the rear of the bike. The FLT's new frame featured a massive rectangular steel backbone, twin downtubes, no centrepost and rear shocks repositioned further away from the swinging arm pivot to permit greater wheel travel. Eureka! With all these improvements in one go, the lighter, more agile handling of FLT felt far superior to the cumbersome Electra Glides.

Early the following year there was also some brilliant news on the company front. A group of Harley employees, members of the founding families and AMF personnel had joined forces, borrowed heavily from the banks and on 26 February 1981, announced they were buying Harley-Davidson Motor Company back from American Machine & Foundry. By June 1981 the eagle was once more standing on its own feet – a cue for celebrations all round, including a poignant York to Milwaukee mass ride-in.

The turbulent but probably life-saving AMF episode behind it, Harley-Davidson made a new commitment to quality, encompassing not just production but the selling and after-service elements of the business. Such spirit was essential as the market for large-capacity motorcycles in America

Above

The enlarged 80 cu in Shovelhead was launched in 1978 in the FLH-80. It featured a full touring package, cast alloy wheels, electronic ignition, a new air cleaner that forced the right knee even further out, and gleaming black cherry paintwork (Mick Woollett)

Right

Even from the rear you could tell the new 1978 model was an 80 incher! The rakish lines of those saddlebags sure looked fine, but made it difficult to house square-shaped objects inside (Mick Woollett)

continued to dwindle. Harley were forced to lay off some workers to make the ship sleeker and better placed to resist the rising influx of big-engined machines exported from Japan.

Stockpiling of these bikes and a slump in H-D's market share to under 25% prompted the company to petition the International Trade Commission to introduce trade tariffs, and in April 1983 President Reagan duly obliged, adding extra taxes on all import motorcycles over 700cc for a five year period. This taste of their own medicine really put the wind up the Japanese. On a happier note, the same year also saw the establishment of the Harley Owners Group, a factory supported club which was aimed at involving riders further in the American marque. Rallies and other events soon provided a focus for owners who had previously felt distanced and disenchanted from the eagle's heart. From a standing start, membership leapt to over 90,000 by the end of the '80s.

By 1983, Harley-Davidson had at last responded to the cries from Electra Glide owners, who fancied the idea of the lower-vibrating, rubber-mounted FLT Tour Glide, but didn't want the bulk of the frame-mounted fairing or its slabby styling. So H-D launched a Tour Glide chassis in an Electra Glide configuration, with the regular handlebar fairing and auxiliary running lights. This FLHT bike used a five-speed transmission and an enclosed final drive chain running in an oil bath, distinguishing it from the FLH Belt Drive Electra Glide which appeared in the model line-up the previous year.

Back in 1978, after undertaking two years research with the Gates

A short run of FLHS-1200 Sport models were manufactured in 1979, weighing 626 lbs dry. The 'undressed' styling heralded both the Electra Glide Sport of the late '80s and Harley's very latest model – the Road King

Rubber Company, Harley had fitted one of its lighter V-twins with a toothed-belt final drive, and the system had proven itself well nigh bulletproof. Here it found its way on to the FLH line-up for the first time, and it's been a good thing ever since. The belt was lighter and less complicated than shaft drive, cheaper to build, more efficient at delivering the engine's power to the rear wheel – Harley claimed 99% – and had none of the handling glitches associated with shaft drive systems.

Devotees of chains were also won over, eventually. The aramid fibre belt was so tough it would give three times the mileage of a chain, ran quieter, cleaner and provided a cushioning shock absorber for smoother gear changes. What's more there was rise or fall of the bike when accelerating or slowing down, the belt needed no lubrication, required checking every 2500 miles or so and only needed retensioning at wide intervals. That's what you call a technical knock-out, I guess. Of the countless Electra Glide pilots Ino 've come across, I've only ever met one guy who's shredded a toothed-belt. I think they made a crazy medal for him.

Police-specification models of the FLH-80 and FLHT-80 appeared for 1983 too, with the traditional sprung single seat. At just 660 lbs without accessories, the belt-drive FLH-80 was almost in the lightweight category. There was even an FLH-80 Police Special motorcycle and sidecar.

More than 60 small but significant refinements had been made to the FLT Tour Glide by 1983, including a flatter perch and lowered suspension, reducing the seat height by an inch and a half. Adjustable floorboards with an inch of movement were now fitted, along with revised

mountings for the saddlebags to facilitate easier removal from the bike. Details you couldn't see improved rider and passenger comfort – vents in the rear fender helped dissipate heat away from the engine, and tubeless tyres also appeared.

Above

This factory photograph of the 1979 FLH 1200 shows just how much the Tour Glide was needed. That Comfort Flex seat waving round in the air looks just plain ridiculous (Harley-Davidson photo)

Left

That's better – an option from 1979 on was a lower frame-mounted saddle that melded smoothly into the bike's proportions and gave a practical 28 inch seat height (Harley-Davidson photo)

1984's Evolution

Having used the Panhead engine for just a year, the Electra Glide then soldiered through almost two decades with Shovelheads before the next stage of its evolution was observed. The Shovelhead had the potential to be both reliable and around 90% oil-tight if properly maintained, but sadly many were not. The final Shovelheads were manufactured in 1984, and a 'new' engine announced to head off customer's increasing irritation with the elderly powerplant of the big V-twins.

The V2 Evolution launched in 1984 was clearly the best V-twin Harley-Davidson had ever produced. With a new aluminium alloy top-end, the Evolution tipped the scales some 20 lbs lighter than its iron-barrelled predecessor, yet made 10% more power and 15% extra torque. A huge number of warranty claims and service problems in the late '70s had forced Harley's hand, and a lengthy five year development period followed to ensure the new motor had better durability and reliability along with increased performance.

To prove the excellence of the Evolution design, Harley-Davidson ran the Evolution on the dynamometer for over 5000 hours and covered three-quarters of a million miles during road testing. To prove the finished product, they even confidently organised a high-speed endurance run at the Alabama International Motor Speedway in Talladega in 1983. Watched by scrutineers from the American Motorcyclists Association, two new bikes – one an FLT Tour Glide – were run virtually non-stop for almost four days.

The objective, to celebrate the company's 80th anniversary, was to let the 80 cu in engine cover 8000 miles at average speeds of 80mph without routine servicing. Harley usually insist that servicing a brand new motorcycle – oil changes and other lubrication – occurs after the first 500 miles, then at 2500, 5000 and 7500 miles, but these weren't included in the speed test.

As the trial was held in the heat of July, this only emphasised the durability of the new engine. Harley actually exceeded their expectations, as both machines averaged 85mph, going faster than the intended speed to allow a margin in case of repairs. None were needed, so the Evolution

'Live to ride' is the legend made possible by the Evolution motor. 'Live to wield lots of spanners' might have been the motto to keep its predecessor, the Shovelhead, on the road and on song

appeared in several big twins in the 1984 model range. Thankfully its nickname 'Blockhead' didn't linger too long, most preferring the term 'Evo'.

To label the Evolution entirely new would be stretching a point, but it's name speaks volumes about Harley-Davidson's philosophy. Dimensions of bore and stroke remained at 88.8 x 108mm, giving the time-honoured displacement of 1340cc/80 cu in. The motor employed the same bottom end and crankshaft as the Shovelhead, though the connecting rods were stronger at the base to improve fatigue life by a factor of ten. There was also a new computer designed camshaft and an improved electronic ignition module.

Up above that, things were very different. Through bolts now held the alloy head and alloy cylinders with SPINY-LOK cast-in iron liners to the crankcase, and the valvetrain had been reworked. New one piece hydraulic lifters were fitted, along with hollow pushrods that fed oil to the rocker shafts and eliminated the need for external oil lines. Being all alloy, the top end now had greater and more even heat dissipation.

Pistons made in Germany by Mahle were actually a few grams lighter than their Shovelhead counterparts, but because they were designed to be perfectly round when working at proper operating temperatures, the engine could be made to closer tolerances, reducing piston slap and increasing power output. This technology wasn't new at the time – it was just new to Harley-Davidson. The flat dome of the piston helped create a new side squish combustion chamber shape, lifting the compression ratio to 8.5:1. Shallower valve angles and taller valves were featured, while smaller, straighter ports also helped improve gas velocity. It all added up to more efficient burning of fuel.

The new engine was available in various dresser configurations for 1984. Rubber-mounted and with a five-speed transmission, the Evo motor was offered in the FLHTC Electra Glide Classic and FLTC Tour Glide models, while a rigid-mounted motor and four-speed box could be had in the FLH Electra Glide and Special Edition versions of the same. All the detailed enhancements to the engine may have been lost on the less technically-minded Harley fans, but every rider could sure as hell feel the difference.

The 10% rise in horsepower to 71.5bhp was realised at a lower 5000rpm engine speed, and meant the bike could gallop along at just under 100mph (although the speedo was only calibrated up to 85mph). More relevant to everyday riding, however, was the news that most of the power was developed in the middle of the rev band. Peak output was now 82.5lbs/ft at 3600rpm, making an Evolution bike less liable to need its gearbox shifting during overtaking manoeuvres. Gas mileages were also up a tad due to the efficient combustion of the motor.

What everyone noticed about the Evo mill was that it had much less of

Above
This tastefully customised 1987 FLHTC may be unique — it's the only example I've heard of where the toothed-belt secondary drive gave up the ghost. Note the disc covers and fork deflectors up at the front

Right
Ball hitches are now quite a common Electra Glide accessory, as their owners seek to tow small trailers to increase luggage capacity

a tendency to spill oil. Little pools and patches of the stuff that were supposed to be inside the engine but were adorning its exterior were the custom for Shovelheads, so the Evolution was something of a novelty in this regard. Just about its only mechanical problem was a random batch of sticking starters early on, cured two years later when the factory increased its cranking power.

For 1984 the FLHTC sported a longer 63 inch wheelbase, a new seat, improved 11.5 inch disc brakes up front and an air suspension/anti-dive system at the top of the forks. Harley were past masters at lifting components from other bikes in their range and using them on other machines. So it was with the anti-dive. A unit which had worked effectively on the previous year's middleweight FXRT, was rescued from the parts bin and added to the Electra Glide.

Whereas other manufacturers resorted to anti-dive systems which

increased damping, reducing but not eliminating dive, Harley went for a method which involved increasing the fork spring rate. A two-stage air chamber was built into the engine guards, with a valve connecting one of the reservoirs to the telescopic forks. When either the front or rear brake was used, a solenoid was activated sealing off a valve and increasing the pressure inside the fork tubes. The beauty of this system was that the rider could change the pressure in the second reservoir and adjust the point at which the valve opened. This meant the front suspension could be individually tailored for ride height, fork travel and softness.

The upturn in Harley's general fortunes and its battle with quality control were revealed when the company won the contract to supply motorcycles to the California Highway Patrol in 1984 – the first time for a decade that a Harley was able to meet this force's rigorous standards. Nor was this a flash in the pan, as the award was repeated in the following years.

Riding impressions of the 1984 FLHTC were strongly favourable, with just a few minor quibbles here and there. The fact that the bike could be started without an ignition key seemed like a bandits' charter unless you remembered to operate the finicky steering lock. Your right knee was still forced out wide by the air cleaner, and the direction indicators only worked when pressure was applied by a digit. That was OK for the highway but trickier if you were trying to make a slow turn, or use the clutch or brake levers at the same time as broadcasting your intended direction.

Depositing yourself behind the adjustable windshield, the FLHTC seemed as wide as ever. To fire her up, you switched on the ignition, pulled the side-mounted choke out, opened the throttle and pressed the button. After the merest hesitation, the Evo motor boomed into life, with plenty of mechanical clatter to accompany the syncopated waffling from the exhausts. Despite the elastomer engine mounts, the Glide shook as much as ever while idling, but the vibes disappeared as soon as you got under way. Carburation from the 38mm single throat Keihin was delightfully clean, enabling the bike to pull strongly after only a brief warm up.

Tweaking the throttle while rolling produced effortless surges in forward velocity, and the engine would only falter if the grip was suddenly cranked wide open while chugging along at very low rpm. The tachometer's redline was set at 5500rpm, but ample power in the mid-

Against a backdrop of Houston office blocks, Patrolmen Tom Barnes radios in to base. 'Yeah, there's this weird guy pointing a lens at me. Shall I let him have it?' Since the California force was won over in 1984, police use of America's only motorcycle marque has increased dramatically

range meant there was no need to even approach this limit. Ideally suited to long open highways, the high gearing meant that at an indicated 60mph the Evo motor was just loping along at a comfortable 2650rpm. Gas mileage when used in this manner is a good 45-50mpg. Peak torque at a lowly 3600rpm also meant fifth gear could be held for longer – you rarely needed to go down to fourth to overtake.

When you do use the gearbox, however, 99 times out of 100 the change of ratio would still be accompanied by a resounding CRRRRASH – enough racket to turn heads and make pedestrians wonder if you'll try the clutch next time. The fun bit, as ever, was trying to get everything to mesh perfectly for that once-in-a-blue-moon silent gearshift. Somehow clutch operation seemed to have got heavier, and the stiffness of its operation could prove a real bind in stop-go traffic. But this was cured later in 1984 when a new diaphragm spring was introduced, giving lighter operation of a clutch now run in oil. This kept it cool and also provided lubricant for the primary chain.

Back out on the open road, the FLHTC felt utterly stable thanks to its lengthy 63 inch wheelbase, so the bike didn't have a tendency to drift off line while you gawked at the scenery. But those same characteristics made tight, low-speed turns still distinctly awkward, the Harley having to be persuaded round corners.

Unlike Electra Glides of old, the 1984 bike with its larger disc pair up front stopped fairly efficiently. Weighing 762lbs with half a tank of gas, it was never going to be the fastest decelerating two-wheeler, but the brakes felt powerful and the lever effort required was light. The less said about the giant rear brake lever they still insisted on fitting the better.

Riding along, sitting behind that stylish fibreglass fairing was still a pleasant place to be, with little buffeting for rider or passenger. The screen could be adjusted for height, and the comfort of the seat was such that hundreds of miles per day were possible, though the riding position remained the typical sit-up-and-beg stance. The wide handlebars were perfectly angled and the instruments in the fork-mounted pod perfectly legible.

A cluster of other subtle modifications appeared on the '84 FLs. The large Tour-Pak was repositioned just over an inch further back, to allow the passenger more room. A switch from Goodyear to lighter Dunlop tyres also helped to keep weight down – this year's FLT was said to have shaved 20 lbs off. Most important of all, new dual disc caliper brakes were included to help stop the rig within respectable distances.

For the 1985 model year, the Tour Glide finally adopted the excellent belt-drive system at the rear, and gained a five-speed transmission to go with it. Other changes to the tourers were limited to air-adjustable rear shock absorbers, revised luggage locks, new silencers and minor cosmetic

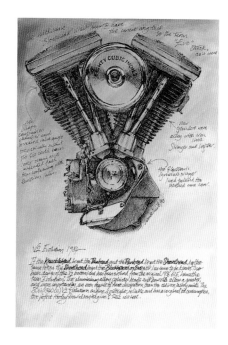

The re-engineered V2 Evolution motor of 1984 was just the tonic Harley-Davidson needed. It's advantages over what had gone before were considerable – more powerful, lighter, cooler and cleaner-running, reliable and oil-tight

For the 1985 model year, the FLT finally gained the dream double – a five-speed gearbox and the toothed-belt drive to the rear wheel (H-D photo)

treatment. Improved disengagement of the starter was afforded by a new relay system.

The policy of numerous if small improvements kept running into 1986 year models. All the tourers switched to the neater 8 inch round air cleaners – less intrusive than the big boxes previously fitted – and sported 2-into-1 exhaust systems. Fairing interiors were revised with increased instrumentation and the option of a factory installed integral sound system complete with handlebar controls. Passengers now had the luxury of floorboards like the rider and, lo and behold, turn signal switches that locked on.

The Way To Go

Fluctuating financial fortunes continued to dog Harley-Davidson in the middle part of the 1980s, despite an increasingly credible model range and the prestige of winning police contracts. There was a certain irony to the situation in 1986, when Milwaukee finally recaptured the No 1 slot back from Honda at the same time as realising the company was technically broke.

The trade tariffs imposed by President Reagan were lifted in early 1987 at Harley's request – a year earlier than expected because the company were confident they could compete on even terms with the Japanese. Floating Harley-Davidson Motor Company on the New York Stock Exchange in July '87 finally secured the company's finances. At the end of that year the sole American marque had captured almost half the domestic heavyweight market.

By 1987 the wheel had turned full circle for Harley's FL range, with the introduction of a 'stripped' Electra Glide for the budget-conscious tourer. The FLHS Sport boasted a 'traditional' windscreen, saddlebags and rack, but no King-Pak top box. This was the cheapest, lightest and most nimble of the 1980s Electra Glides – it's dry weight was a mere 692 lbs.

The big news for the 1989 model year was Harley's launch of luxury, Ultra Classic versions of the Electra Glide and Tour Glide. Their specifications were enhanced by goodies such as special paint schemes, removable fairing lowers with stowage compartments, electronic cruise control and a CB radio and high-spec sound system. The rear speakers had their own 40-watt amplifier and a duplicate set of sound systems controls was afforded the passenger – you can't have enough of a good thing, after all.

Harley pilots had been adding sound to their tourers for years, but the factory-fitted system on the Ultras were something else. Designed for use specifically on a motorcycle, it could withstand the considerable vibration produced by the big V-twin and, with its Lexan one-piece cover, anything the weather could throw at it. The few control buttons were larger than

Having had Yamahas previously, Horatio – a police border guard from Texas – finally took the plunge and treated himself to his first Harley at the age of 41. You get the impression that he's pleased with his 1992 Electra Glide Sport. With a 'police' screen the FLHS weighs 692lbs, has 82.5bhp on tap and can rumble up to about 110mph

usual to make operation by a gloved hand easy.

Elsewhere, evidence of Harley's continuing commitment to detailed quality improvement was seen by the fact that an upgraded material without a fibreglass-like pong was now used for the saddlebags. On the mechanical front, all the 1340cc tourers got an uprated 32 amp alternator, and the electric starter was revamped for the nth time – a new 1.2 kw direct-drive system at last put paid to odd gremlins affecting the electric leg. Harley finally found a fix for the turn signal mess too by fitting self-cancelling switches controlled by a microprocessor that monitored both speed and distance.

Naturally all the extra bibs and bobs on these luxury liners did little for their figures. Compared to the trim 692 lbs dry weight of the no-frills FLHS, the Ultra version of the FLTC bent the scales with a dry figure of 784 lbs. Indeed weight watching is one of the fascinating aspects of the

Adding a pair of legshields and changing the fibreglass fairing for the windshield has made this FLHTC Classic into a distinctive tourer. The latest accessory catalogue provides countless permutations of parts, providing your wallet is deep enough

Glide dynasty.

Back in the '50s Harley had a big twin tourer. First the swinging arm added around 80lbs to an already large motorcycle, while the 1965 machine with its starter, larger battery and extra wiring put on a further 75lbs. The first Shovelheads weighed 783lbs with a half tank of fuel and could manage 98mph, despite only pumping out some 60bhp from its 74 cu ins. A California-spec Electra Glide of the 1990s has a potentially beefier motor but actually has a slightly lower top speed, thanks to the constricting effects of all those emissions regulations!

As the Electra Glide rolled into the current decade, only a further series of detail changes were apparent, showing that Harley's stable of big tourers had come about as far as they could. A reworked clutch was added to the '90 bikes, and voice-activated intercoms to reduce background noise appeared for 1991 models along with vibration-isolated floorboards. Specially developed Dunlop Elite tyres also promised up to 50% more miles.

For 1992, all FLs sported a recalibrated 40mm carburettor to improve cold start performance, continuously vented fuel tanks for smoother delivery of fuel and new brake and disc material for better stopping. Most striking of all were the new powder coat paint schemes – a result of the company's massive £45 million investment on improved production facilities. The new paint plant had 90,000 square feet of floor space, a squeaky clean environment and an array of robot sprayers. Colour changes which took a whole day were now completed in ten seconds, and the paint had a quality and consistency never seen before in the company's history.

A slight rejig at the rear of the frame in '93 saw the oil tank depart to under the gearbox and permitted a more central location for the battery. Shifting these two items meant that the right hand pannier now had a decent internal capacity. Both saddlebags featured new, hinged lids to replace the archaic tongue and groove set-up that had been there from day one. New for 1994 was the FLHR Electra Glide Road King, with styling similar to the FLHS it replaced in the line-up, except that the seat could be quickly converted into a studded solo affair. That and no rack at the rear gave it a lean look harking back to 1979 – there'd been a bare FLHS-1200 'Sport' fitted with a police screen briefly during the late '70s,

So what lies ahead for the Electra Glide? After a quarter of a century of production and painstakingly gradual evolution, the King of the Road has long been overtaken by faster and more efficient machines. None approach it for character or tradition, of course – those are the Harley's main virtues, yet they are also its weaknesses. Hidebound by a philosophy that glances back at what's been achieved as much as it peers gingerly forward into the future, the company faces a dilemma. Progress must continue but if anything too outlandish is produced, Harley risks upsetting the marque's

As a test bed for noise and emission experiments, Harley created the 'Batmobile' in the early '90s and weren't afraid to show it. Increasingly punitive noise legislation is making the air-cooled V-twin harder to run effectively

vast, loyal following. And that's always assuming Milwaukee has the
resources to do so, because Hammamatsu it ain't.

The crux of the problem is the veteran V-twin, which ironically is about
as efficient as it could be in this guise and vastly superior to its forebears.
Remember the 1340cc/80 cu in V2 Evolution of the 1990s is based on a
design that can trace a clear ancestry back to 1936 – the 61E
'Knucklehead' of 1000cc/61 cu in, and even that probably wasn't a clean
sheet design. Throughout the '80s and '90s, the Evolution has been
strangled more and more by increasingly punitive noise and emissions
legislation. Given this scenario, can the air-cooled V-twin as we know it
survive?

Rumours have circulated for years that Harley-Davidson has conducted
trials with another engine, probably of water-cooled design to increase
power yet reduce noise. Like UFOs, numerous sightings have been claimed
and reports in the American motorcycle press even admitted that a V-4
prototype had actually been shown to selected dealers as long ago as 1984
– apparently the first time anyone outside factory personnel had seen the
motor in the metal. Over a decade later it's still not in production, but
another motor most certainly is.

Just in time for 1994's Daytona 200, the VR1000 was unveiled – a lusty
four-stroke V-twin just like Milwaukee's first competition racer back in
1916. Its specification, however, is like no Harley before, with a 60° angle
between the water-cooled cylinders, and an oversquare bore and stroke of
98mm x 66mm giving a capacity of 1000cc/61 cu in. The VR1000 has an

upper limit approaching 11000rpm, fuel injection, four-valve heads and is claimed to unleash over 140 horses.

Though its first outings have been disappointing, the VR1000 shows that Harley-Davidson isn't afraid of radical design. But this engine seems a far cry from the traditional V-twin and it's unclear what ramifications, if any, the current racer programme has for future road machines. The company makes little attempt to conceal its racing ambitions, knowing the vast prestige that can be gained from winning a world championship.

What adds spice to the project is that to compete in any of the major series, in America or abroad, Harley must comply with homologation rules. These state that at least 50 road-going versions of the bike must also be built. It's surely unlikely that a big tourer would be part of these plans, but there may be spin-offs ultimately. Tradition or not, anything is possible if Harley has to comply with even stricter future legislation. So what form will the Electra Glide take as it approaches the millennium, and Harley's own centenary soon after? Can the time-honoured V-twin keep thumping on, or will we see a water-cooled King of the Road? How about a V4 Electra Glide? Now there's a couple of bikes to conjure with.

Leaving conjecture aside, there are still some voices who maintain that Harley-Davidson took a wrong turn with the Electra Glide's evolutionary route in the early '80s. The bike that's been produced for the last decade, they maintain, is no more than an FLT Tour Glide dressed-up to look like an Electra Glide, so how about giving the tourer the independent identity it deserves. That would leave the FLT to take on the Gold Wing, and let the Electra Glide return to its roots.

Perhaps they have a point, though having come this far surely there's no way Harley-Davidson could reinvent the bike. Then again, being past masters at delving into the parts bin, and turning back the clock, perhaps Milwaukee have already thought about it, basing a tourer on the excellent Dyna Glide chassis, say?

Only the present band of H-D executives actually know what's round the corner, and we can only look where the tourer has been and where it is now. A common thread runs through those thirty years, concerning all the people who've bought one. The Electra Glide is for riders who prefer to be able to see and hear a motorcycle's engine and feel it at work, riders who want some touring luxuries but not blandness, and riders who believe that just because a technology is a few years or even decades old doesn't mean to say it's obsolete. To all these people the Harley-Davidson Electra Glide is an amalgam of a certain style and tradition redolent of America, and therein lies the bike's strongest appeal.

Above
Yet another anniversary model in special silver and black paint, this time to celebrate Harley's 90 years of motorcycle production in 1993. Small perspex screens added to the handlebar fairing to help keep air from the rider's lower torso and knees

Right
Ultra version of the Electra Glide has beautifully detailed legshields but they're not as effective as the Tour Glide fairing. For laid back highway cruising, note the highway pegs attached to the crash bars

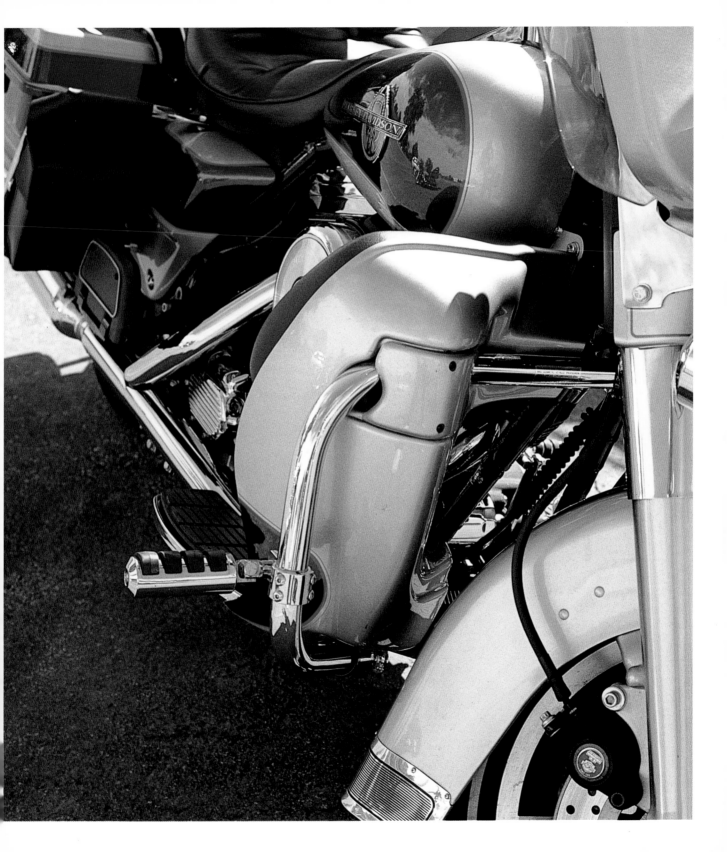

Right

At speed, the 1994 Ultra Classic Electra Glide is an impressive sight, though lean angles are still restricted. Still, who wants to hurry on a bike like this? (MCN)

Overleaf

The latest in a long line of Electra Glides stretching back 30 years is the FLHR Road King for the 1994 model year. Again it's a mixture of tradition and invention, with a detachable seat section and windshield enhancing its retro styling. The oil tank now resides below and behind the gearbox, enabling the battery to move and give more room inside the right hand pannier (MCN)

Above

Echoes of 1979 were apparent in 1987, when the Electra Glide Sport was launched. Shorn of the King Pak and wearing a windshield instead of the fibreglass fairing, it found immediate popularity (Harley-Davidson photo)

Right

Eventually, Harley get round to sorting out something that's bothered you for years, and in 1993 it was the old saddlebag lids. Now they open to the side, courtesy of a sturdy, chrome-plated hinge and hidden retaining strap

Overleaf

No mistaking the broad-as-an-armchair Electra Glide profile as the 1994 FLHR hustles through the twisties (MCN)